THE BORED BOOK

155 Things To Do

VIKKI LAWRENCE

THE BORED BOOK
155 THINGS TO DO

Dedicated to:

My Sweet Son, Miss Copper and Other Friends
who are a great source of Information and Inspiration

Paperback
ISBN 13: 978-1-885615-78-7
ISBN: 1-885615-78-7

Kindle
ISBN 13: 978-1-885615-79-4
ISBN: 1-885615-79-5

Copyright © 2015-2020 Vikki Lawrence

Published by: Vikki Lawrence Publishing

All rights reserved. This book (electronic file/ebook OR hard-copy OR audio) or any part thereof may not be reproduced in any form whatsoever, whether by graphic, visual, electronic, filing, microfilming, tape recording or any other means, except in the case of brief passages embodied in critical reviews and articles, without the prior written permission of the publisher.

NOTICE: This guide is intended for informational purposes only and should be used as a supplement only. Author and Publisher are not medically-trained, and are not responsible or liable for the misuse or use of any information contained herein. The information contained in this book is true and complete and accurate to the best of our knowledge. All suggestions and recommendations are made without any guaranty on the part of the writer or publishers. We disclaim any liability incurred in connection with the use of this information.

Vikki Lawrence

THE BORED BOOK
155 THINGS TO DO

TABLE OF CONTENTS

Chapter One: You Are Sooo Bored!...4
Chapter Two: The List Of Things To Do...................................5
Chapter Three: Activity Pages...50
More Books 92
About The Author 93
Contact Information 94
Five Year Prep Journals / Diaries..95
Blank Five-Year Journals / Diaries 96
Writing Prompt Books...98
Five-Year Seizure Diaries / Trackers 99
Notes 100

CHAPTER ONE: YOU ARE SOOO BORED!

Life is unpredictable. You could be going along, celebrating the birth of a new year, and WHAM! The All-of-Humanity is knocked on its collective hind-ends. Or a blizzard has been raging around your home for days, and now you are cut off from the world by six-foot-tall snow drifts. Or a hurricane came ashore and washed away all infrastructure.

You could be confined or quarantined (whether self-imposed or government/health organization) for 3 days, a week, two, or even a month or two. Or year. If things get really bad, you might not have electricity to watch videos or TV or get on the internet. What do you plan on doing with your day?

I have a solar-charger for tablets and phones, so assuming books and games are loaded directly onto my tablet, I can read and play games for a few hours each day. However, I also like to write (on the computer or on paper), work on puzzles and word finds, garden on my tiny patio, bake, make jams from scratch, help my special needs son with his own writings, sing, play the keyboard, and paint by numbers or sun-catchers.

The next section gives 155 suggestions for how to pass your time.

Note: This paperback version has more information than the Kindle/e-book version.

CHAPTER TWO: THE LIST OF THINGS TO DO

Besides playing games (online and off, real-time or virtual), watching TV and videos, and eating... here is the list I've compiled of possible things to do when you are confined for a length of time.

1. READ books that you have been meaning to get to.... some day. Peruse a thrift or book store. Borrow from the library (physical or digital/online). Download onto your tablet / e-reader from an online provider. Include those really long books, like "Gone With The Wind", "Pride and Prejudice", or "The Odyssey." Here are a some other suggestions:

    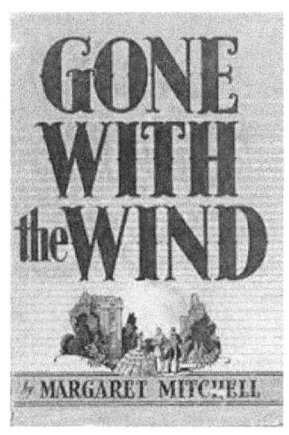

    1) 1984
    2) A Midsummer Night's Dream
    3) A Separate Peace
    4) A Tale of Two Cities
    5) All Quiet on the Western Front
    6) Animal Farm
    7) Antigone
    8) Beloved
    9) Beowulf
    10) Brave New World
    11) Charlotte's Web
    12) Crime and Punishment
    13) Death of a Salesman
    14) Fahrenheit 451
    15) Great Expectations
    16) Hamlet
    17) Harry Potter (series)

18) Jane Eyre
19) Little Women
20) Lord of the Flies
21) Macbeth
22) Number the Stars
23) Of Mice and Men
24) Romeo and Juliet
25) The Adventures of Huckleberry Finn
26) The Adventures of Tom Sawyer
27) The Awakening
28) The Book Thief
29) The Canterbury Tales
30) The Catcher in the Rye
31) The Crucible
32) The Diary of a Young Girl (Anne Frank)
33) The Giver
34) The Grapes of Wrath
35) The Great Gatsby
36) The Hobbit
37) The Hunger Games (series)
38) The Iliad
39) The Metamorphosis
40) The Lord of the Rings
41) The Old Man and the Sea
42) The Outsiders
43) The Scarlet Letter
44) The Stranger
45) The Things They Carried
46) To Kill A Mockingbird
47) Wuthering Heights

2. START a college fund for each of your children. Many banks will let you do this online. Even if your child is already in high school, it is rarely too late to start saving. Encourage your child to also contribute it by getting a job, even if it is just babysitting or washing cars.

3. SKYPE / facetime / zoom to have a "face-to-face" conversation with someone without actually being face-to-face.

4. WORK on standing up for yourself. No need to be a jerk about it, but sometimes a gentle 'no' can work magic. Suggestions how:

   1) Stand up for your time. It's yours.

   2) Be deliberate with your words and actions.

   3) Practice being transparent and authentic.

   4) Figure out what's really bothering you.

   5) Take powerful but small steps.

   6) Practice makes perfect.

   7) Clarify first, as to what you are being asked (or request/required) to do. Don't attack. Just ask.

   8) When someone attacks, wait them out. Eventually they will have to take a breath!

   9) There is a somewhat new trend calling entitled women "Karen". It got its origin on the Reddit website in 2017 when a user's ex-wife, Karen, took the man for everything during the divorce, including his children. His posts led to the creation of a 'subreddit" and from there, the use of "Karen" went on to mean a demanding, entitled and inappropriate woman who uses aggressive behavior when prevented from getting her way. I bring this up here because a "Karen" can run over even the most strong of people.

Practice how you would respond to entitled people who try to push you into doing their bidding.

5. PRIDE in your work, in your garden, in your parenting … these are all ok things to be proud about. Value your contributions to humanity.

6. FAMILY trees can be complicated, there are many websites to help you track your genealogy, including:
   1) www.ancestry.com
   2) www.myheritage.com/genealogy
   3) www.genealogy.com/genealogy/records
   4) www.archives.com
   5) www.familysearch.org
   6) www.findmypast.com
   7) www.myheritage.com
   8) www.23andme.com
   9) and more. I have also published a 'Family History Workbook' (www.amazon.com/dp/1885615094) to help you create a record to pass down to future generations. Besides the obvious family tree pages, it  includes places to list medical histories, family reunions, heirlooms, traditions, and recording family stories. There are plenty of pages for photographs too (always a good idea to have a printed out picture in case digital copies get corrupted).

7. CONSTRUCTIVE criticism can be hard to take. Work on how to take it in the spirit it is given. (There are, of course, people who SAY they are giving constructive criticism but in reality just want to mock, degrade or condemn. If you can't tell the difference between the first and the second, learn!)

8. WRITE a bucket list. What have you always wanted to do but didn't have the time to do? Paint? Learn to carve a toy out of a piece of wood? See how high you can sing? Wear an evening gown or tuxedo? This book should give you lots of ideas, and even more suggestions follow:

    1) Attend the Olympics,
    2) Be in a parade, hold the ropes for a parade balloon, or ride on a parade float.
    3) Catch a foul ball at a major league game.
    4) Go bungee jumping or sky-diving.
    5) Grow the biggest pumpkin on record.
    6) Ride a mechanical bull at its fastest level.
    7) Ride an elephant across the Sarengeti.
    8) Ride horses in a forest, on the Scottish moors, or on a beach.
    9) Take a hot air balloon ride.
    10) Visit a wild animal sanctuary.

9. RESEARCH Guinness World Records (GWR), and set one yourself. Did you know there is a GWR Day? It is "an annual celebration of record-breaking, a day which sees thousands of people around the world come together with one common goal, to become a title holder." See: *www.guinnessworldrecords.com* to get some ideas.

10. PLAN a two-week vacation for just yourself. Then when you can, go!

11. IDENTIFY your strengths and weaknesses. Be brutally honest. Then figure out how to change your weaknesses into strengths, or work on the improving your weaknesses. Examples:

1) Strengths: versatility, determination, enthusiasm, patience, creativity, honesty, discipline, trustworthiness, respectfulness and dedication.

2) Weaknesses: Impatience, trouble saying 'no', lack of experience, hard-headedness, trouble asking for help, hard time letting go, hard time admitting you are wrong, lack of confidence, and lack of specific skills.

12. COMPLIMENT a co-worker, family member or stranger every day. You might just be giving a boost to take someone's day from yuck to yum.

13. CREATE a piece of art for your home. Paint, collage, melted crayons… there are many mediums to choose from. Look around to see what kind of supplies you can find, even the things you might originally overlook. Suggestions: pebbles, pine needles, sand, buttons, dryer lint, and even chia seeds.

14. JOURNAL about something … anything … daily! There are many blank journals available in most bookstores, online and in person. You can even use a plain ole spiral notebook. What should you write about? Feelings. Poetry. Arguments. Random thoughts. Or you could use a journal to track things like exercise, blood sugar readings, food/drink eaten, or even seizures.

15. LEARN to cook a super-extravagant dish / meal. Not  sure how to do this? Browse through recipes that sound interesting, then watch cooking shows online, including YouTube. Write out on a piece of paper (yes, old school) the recipe, as this will help you understand the instructions. Double-check that you

wrote the recipe correctly. Buy enough ingredients to make it twice, just in case you mess up the first time. When you are ready to prepare the dish, get all of your ingredients prepared (prepped) first. Take your time, reading and re-reading the recipe as you go through the steps. When the dish is ready, have someone taste-test it with you.

16. WHAT is your personal brand? From Wikipedia, "personal branding is the conscious and intentional effort to create and influence public perception of an individual by positioning them as an authority in their industry, elevating their credibility, and differentiating themselves from the competition, to ultimately advance their career, increase their circle of influence and have a larger impact." This has become .a huge practice, especially with YouTube, TikTok and other social media, and "influencers". So, if you have a personal brand, what is it? Write it out.

17. LIST your fears, then work towards conquering them. Here are a few common fears:

   1) Fear of being alone
   2) Fear of being confined
   3) Fear of blood
   4) Fear of bugs
   5) Fear of dogs
   6) Fear of enclosed or crowded spaces
   7) Fear of flying
   8) Fear of getting a disease
   9) Fear of heights
   10) Fear of lightning
   11) Fear of needles
   12) Fear of snakes
   13) Fear of spiders

14) Fear of the dark
15) Fear of thunder
16) Fear of water

18. TRAIN (yes, even indoors) to run a marathon. Sometimes, when I am stuck inside, I walk real fast, back and forth in the biggest room of my home. It does get a little boring, but when I put on some good tunes, it helps make the time (and laps) go faster.

19. LEARN to play chess, checkers, or backgammon. Whether you know nothing about these games, or haven't played since childhood, there are ways to play online with people of all types of experience.

20. TAKE a job that allows you to travel. Obviously, start it as soon as you are not confined or quarantined. Suggestions: cruise ship worker, flight attendant, pilot, travel agent, customer service agent, foreign service officer, military, consultant, English-as-a-second-language teacher, journalist, tour guide, au pair (nanny), travel or hospitality writer, and last but certainly not least…any job you can do online, you can do on a beach in Tahiti or on a balconey in Venice, Italy.

21. GARDENING can be so relaxing, and is very rewarding, especially if you grow food or herbs. Even if you have only a small corner in your tiny apartment, you can have a few pots for carrots, salad greens including spinach, parsley and chives. If you have an outdoor balcony or patio, like I do (for now!), you could have a few pots 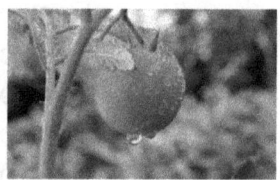 of tomatoes, jalapeno peppers, blueberries, strawberries, green beans and even marigolds (the petals ARE edible). And if you own a place with a yard,

in addition to growing some fruits and veggies in the ground or in pots or raised beds, you could also plant a few nut trees (the smallest would probably be a filbert/hazelnut) or fruit trees, and maybe some berry brambles.

22. TV SHOWs in a foreign language can be educational. Some people use this as a way to learn that different language! Or you can watch, and make up your own dialogue in your native tongue.

23. LEARN how to do your own taxes. If you are so inclined, become certified to do other people's taxes. It would be a good source of income, from home, for several months out of the year.

24. TAKING INVENTORY of your possessions is something most people don't bother with. However, if you have a  fire or other disaster, and have a complete list, it will make filing a claim with your homeowner's or renter's insurance company a little easier. Make an accounting of what you have and where. From food to paper products to tools, books, art supplies and electrical cords. As you take inventory, re-organize what goes where, and also be sure to take a LOT of pictures of especially the most valuable items you possess.

25. RISKS can be scary, but can offer huge rewards. Take a CALCULATED risk in work, at home, with hobbies, whatever. Try out-of-the-box ideas.

26. LEARN a language. Some to choose from: Japanese, Spanish, German, Portuguese, Italian, and Sign Language.

27. POETRY has been around for nearly four-thousand years. It is written to share ideas, create imagery and express emotion. Even more than in fiction, poets use words specifically for how they sound, the number of syllables, their meaning, and how they can create a particular rhythm or tempo. Some types use rhyming, ending two or more lines that end in like-sounding words. Poetry is an important part of culture and art, even in these modern days. Here are a few kinds of poems:

    1) Blank verse
    2) Epic
    3) Free verse / freeform
    4) Haiku
    5) Limerick
    6) Narrative
    7) Pastoral
    8) Sonnet

28. ORGANIZE your home. Can't find lids in your kitchen? Time to organize your pots and pans, your storables, and utensils. The following are a few ideas to get you started:

    1) Start with storage spaces. This way, as you move through your home going from room to room, you will have storage areas all sorted out. For instance, if you decide you won't be using your bread machine again until next year, you can pack it away in a good storage area until you are ready to use it again. Maybe start small with clearing out a junk drawer, then the junk/hall closet, and then a big room in your basement. Break up larger spaces into smaller spaces.

2) Move on to 'shared spaces'. Start with the kitchen, then the entrance hall/foyer, living room and then the bathrooms. Don't forget the outside deck, porch or patio. Seeing these spaces organized will give you a boost of confidence, and a sense of peace. This might even spill over to the rest of the people you live with.

3) Next, organize the personal spaces like your bedroom, closet and home office. Do the closet before tackling the bedroom because closets tend to spill out of their confinement. These types of spaces may take a little longer, especially the office, because you will need to look at each paper to decide whether to toss, handle or file.

4) Finally, you are left with smaller spaces, like a laundry room, linen closet, mudroom and guest rooms. Not sections you would normally dedicate much thought to, these areas are important to how you family can function.

29. GET a college degree. Some colleges and universities offer reduced rates to those who qualify.

30. MAKE a video that goes viral on TikTok, FaceBook, Instagram or YouTube.

31. CARVING candles is a beautiful skill that can be well worth the time it takes to learn and do.  Candles in a long star-shaped are dipped multiple times in various colored wax, then while still quite warm, are carved to create beautiful masterpieces.

32. SOAP-making can be a very rewarding activity. There are many kits available to make many kinds of soap. Watch a few videos on the how-to's and get started. Be sure to take precautions because you will be working with very hot ingredients, and in some cases, caustic elements like lye.

33. CARDS, like regular playing cards, Uno^{tm}, etc, are an excellent way to pass the time. Remember to pick up a book on different card games.

34. MEDITATATION can help your blood pressure, your heart rate, and your ability to deal with stress, among other things. It is the best time to learn how to calm your mind and body. Sit crosslegged quietly, or lay down with eyes closed, palms up. Focus on your breathing. Say or think a soothing word over and over.

35. TELL someone how much they have inspired you. Be sincere and thankful.

36. COLORING…it isn't just for kids! There are a lot of coloring books specifically made for adults, including zentangles. These are more complex than those for children. If you don't want to limit yourself to a box of 64-colors of crayons, consider getting

colored pencils, gel pens, maybe even chalk or watercolors. There is no rule that says the pages HAVE to stay in the book! Use an easel if you desire to paint the pictures instead of color. Or find tiny shells, colored sand or other items to glue onto the sheet. Use this as a time to be super-creative. And remember… no one is judging you!

37. MANICURES (fingernails) and pedicures (toenails) are something that can help pass the time. If you haven't done them yourself, there are plenty of tutorials online, or FaceTime a friend and do them "together'! Don't ignore giving these beauty-treatments to your children, or having them do them on you…guys included!

38. LEARN something new about your job's industry. Find a good (current) book, either online or from the library, that gives a lot of information. Dedicate time each day to read a chapter or two. When you finish that book, get another. You can also take online courses.

39. BUILD up a rainy-day / emergency fund. Do you just throw your change into a jar, or on top of your dresser? Does it get lost in your handbag? Find a big jar in a thrift store (or dollar store), decorate it, and begin adding your change to it. Do you sell eggs, or cookies? That money can go in there too.

40. WRITE a love letter. It doesn't have to be for a romantic interest. Consider writing to your parent, sibling, child or even a favorite teacher from high school. There are several journals you can use to write love letters to your significant other:
    1) www.amazon.com/dp/b084p574tr
    2) www.amazon.com/dp/b084dg2wqg
    3) www.amazon.com/dp/b084nlbhp7

4) www.amazon.com/dp/b084qbl6k1
5) www.amazon.com/dp/b084p6ghw4

41. TREAT your skin. With what you have on hand, create a spa in your home. Make an oatmeal mask, or place cucumber slices over your eyes. Steam-bath your face and moisturize with whatever you come up with by searching online.

42. VISION boards came into popularity several years ago.  Cut out pictures from magazines, or print out pictures or words. Arrange them on a corkboard or big piece of poster board or even across your bedroom wall. The vision board will be a huge visual reminder every day of the goals you plan to attain.

43. READ five books on budgeting, frugal spending, and healthy finances. Take notes and come up with a plan to implement suggestions that could help your finances. There is no need to spend money for these books. Go to your library, but if it is closed, you might be able to borrow e-books online from them. You could also find e-books from other sources.

44. MAKEUP expires. Do you have cosmetics that are older than six months? Time to throw them out. Don't draw on your eyebrows any more? Toss out the pencils.

45. TEACH a workshop on online about something you are really good at. If you don't know how to do that, google "where can I give an online workshop", or "how can I develop an online workshop".

46. WHO makes you happy? Or contributes to your happiness? Surround yourself with people who you feel good about, and who do the same for you. Life is too short to be with people who are always crabby, and who always seem to find a way to make your miserable. And, yes, that can include family. Just… be happy.

47. BOARD games are a great time-filler. Play games like Monopoly^{tm}, Scrabble^{tm}, Candyland^{tm}, etc. Now is the time to actually read those really long and complicated instructions.

48. PLAN to go skinny dipping, then when you have the opportunity… do it! Um… don't get caught.

49. WORKPLACE conflicts can make doing your job very difficult. Managers who go on power trips. Subordinates gunning for your job. Co-workers who are just mean, or lazy, or shiftless. Learn how to deal with them.

50. FIND an animal sanctuary near you (elephant, big cat, lizards, whatever). These places promise to take in and care for animals that have been abandoned, abused and/or neglected, and to keep them for the rest of their lives. They take into consideration conservation needs, potential for scientific research, and what species most needs help in their area. They exist mostly on donations from patrons, government grants, and people "adopting" specific animals. Become a patron. Donate for their upkeep. Plan to visit when you can.

51. PLAN an entire month of "no spending" money except for regular absolutely-required expenses.

52. PROJECT kits, like to make lip gloss, a dream catcher, tie quilts, painting sun catchers or paint-by-numbers, can really fill the time. As a side benefit, the end results can be given as gifts.

53. THERAPY doesn't have to be sitting for 50 minutes with a shrink or therapist. Try meditation, yoga, reiki, acupuncture, acupressure, chanting, or some other relaxing pastime. A good long honest talk with a friend can also work wonders, especially if you have a person who is honest back with you and is willing to listen and give a shoulder to be cried upon.

54. SEW a face mask, apron, headband, baby blanket, tote or grocery bag, or … ?? You could even make new curtains for your kitchen, or throw pillows for your couch.

55. REDECORATE your home. If you are getting bored silly by looking at your home day in and day out, consider redecorating. Try a new paint color as an accent wall. Recover your couch or slip-cover your dining room chairs. Turn your comforter the other way (if each side is different). Make a new quilt to add a homey-ness to your bedroom. Paint your front door red, or purple. Draw a design on your mailbox. If you rent, there are wallpapers that can be put up and taken down with no damage to walls.

56. CERTIFICATIONS all up-to-date for your job? If you aren't current, use this time to get them done. Want a

bump in pay or job status? Work on getting the certifications for those.

57. HAIR styles change so quickly so if you are bored, take this time to try something new. You don't necessarily have to cut your hair, but you can try a different part, or curl, or straighten, or even change the color. For people going through chemotherapy, gather up a bunch of scarves and try different head-wrap styles, or different hats for you gents.

58. ORGANIZE your receipts by type then by date, and keep separated in envelopes, plastic baggies or file folders. Whatever works for you. Create a spreadsheet (computer or on paper) with columns delineating categories like home office, donations, medical expenses, etc. Remember to include a column (or a separate sheet) for all of your income.

59. SUNCATCHERS are a fun and easy way to pass the time. There are many kits for painting suncatchers, plus, you can also make your own.

60. EMBROIDERY is becoming a lost art. Get an embroidery kit and teach yourself how to do it, with special embroidery floss (thread), beautiful patterns and designs with special stitches and knots. I haven't done this for years, and think I just might take it up again! *Note: Embroidery can be done by either women OR men!*

61. MAKE time for yourself each and every day, even if it is just a ten-minute bubble-bath, playing on your handheld game unit, or putting a few more pieces in that huge jigsaw puzzle.

62. LEARN how to play an instrument (or practice one you haven't picked up in a while). Make sure not to bother your neighbors....or give a recital at dusk from your front door.

63. PLAN to be in the studio audience of a TV show.

64. EXPERIMENT with making your dog's food yourself. A good recipe for my last dog (purebred Labrador retriever) was: 1/4 cooked brown rice, 1/4 cooked eggs, 1/4 cooked meat like turkey, and 1/4 cooked veggies like sweet potatoes or carrots. He loved it!

65. WHITTLE a piece of hard wood. How cool would it be to sit on your front porch, in an old-timey rocking chair, whittling from a piece of wood with a kitchen paring knife. The things you carve are limited only by your imagination: toy, whistle, bust of a famous person, car with working wheels, a tree or flower, a butterfly, a bear, and so on.

66. CLEAN your house from top to bottom. Literally. The attic and its spiders, and all the way down to the basement and crawl spaces. Sweep, mop, dust, launder and clean every surface, fabric, window and screen.

Don't ignore the outside of windows and doors, and if you can, powerwash (without causing damage) your house's exterior, decks and porches. Now would also be a good time to slap on a fresh coat of paint.

67. GRATITUDE is missing from our daily lives. Don't wait for a special day like Thanksgiving, or going to church ... focus on being grateful in every day of your life.

68. EAT only plant-based foods for a week. Take a "meatless Monday" and extend it through seven days. If you aren't sure you will be getting enough protein, look up online "vegan sources of protein". Some are: nuts, seeds, grains, beans, chickpeas / garbanzo beans / hummus, peas, lentils, peanuts, soybeans / tofu (get non-gmo, please), nutritional yeast, spelt, teff, quinoa, hempseed, and amaranth.

69. EXTEND your plant-based diet for a week ... into two weeks, and maybe even a month.

70. WRITE your will. There are kits and forms online that can help you. Work out where your kids would go upon your death. Set up a trust, if necessary. Decide who would get your jewelry or heirlooms. Maybe a local high school's home ec program benefit from getting all of your fabric and sewing paraphernalia, or the whole of your kitchen set up.  A local library would probably love to receive your extensive collection of DVDs or books. Be sure to get the will executed and notarized as soon as possible, with a copy going to your Executor and/or people you trust. Remember, it is absolutely nobody's

business what's in your will, except telling your children's guardians-to-be that they will be such, and you do need the Executor's okay to take the job. (While you're at it, write out and execute a Living Will, Power of Attorney, and whatever else is necessary.)

According to https://www.legalzoom.com/articles/making-a-will-a-quick-checklist, your will should include the following:

1) Beneficiaries (people who will inherit real and/or personal property from you). You don't necessarily have to say who gets what; just focus on not forgetting anyone. If you wish to disinherit a spouse or children, you need to look up the laws in your area, as some might not allow that.

2) Assets can include big things like businesses, vehicles, and houses, and then work your way down to the littler things, like jewelry or family heirlooms. Some things can't be included in a will but at this point, just get down everything you can think of.

3) Debts include student loan, mortgage, liens, car loans, credit cards, outstanding taxes and so on. You won't be leaving these to anyone but these need to be listed so you can get an idea of where your finances are so you can make plans, including your funeral. Note: debts that will be a responsibility of your estate should be covered by a life insurance policy so you might want to take one out now.

4) Deciding who will be your Executor/Executrix is important. This person will make sure your will is followed, and must be noted in the will. The person (and the alternate in case of non-availability) should be ok with being chosen.

5) If you have minor children, you need to choose their guardians. This is especially important if the other parent is unavailable (or dies at the same time) or unfit, and if your child is an adult but can't handle his/her affairs. *(My 23 year old son is mentally about 10 years old, and can't handle his own affairs due to his autism and the epilepsy that has created havoc in his brain.)* You will also need to decide how your children will be cared for (financially), and at what age they will be able to inherit.

71. KITTENS and PUPPIES are the subject of many hilarious videos online. I dare you not to "ooh" , "aah" or giggle. And it really is a great way to relax and unwind. Give it a try!

72. FIND a way to love the job you have. If you can't, find a job you love.

73. LEARN a new software program, like PhotoShop, Opera GX, Postbox, Calibre or Etcher. You could also learn how to use the apps on your phone!

74. SUPPORT a cause that means a great deal to you… fighting spousal abuse, pet spaying / neutering, child neglect, etc. Supporting a cause doesn't necessarily mean giving money. It could be you volunteering your time, doing advertising or marketing from home, printing flyers, or even organizing a fundraiser.

75. TAKE time to appreciate the outdoors. Even if you are confined inside, you can have a potted plant (flower, vegetable, fern … you choose!).

76. PAY off all of your student loan debt and credit cards. If the interest rate is 23%, compounded monthly, then consider getting a loan at 5% to pay off the debt with the higher interest rate. Get the advice of a respectable accountant or financial advisor.

77. PLAN a yard / garage / tag sale for the Summer or Autumn. Start going through every inch of your home, putting things to sell in boxes with prices already marked. Keep an inventory of what's in the box. Trust me… it will make preparing for the yard sale so much easier. Bonus Tip: If you have the garage sale on a hot day, you can boost your traffic and sales by selling cold water bottles or lemonade. Cool or cold day? Try hot cocoa. People like to buy other goodies like cookies and cupcakes too.

78. REQUEST a free copy of your credit report. If the score isn't high enough, make a plan (and implement it) to make your score excellent.

79. COOK all of your meals for one week straight. Then try it for two weeks straight. Can't cook? There are many many cooking shows online and on YouTube.

80. START a vacation fund. Whether a weekend at a bed-and-breakfast, or a month-long cruise (cough), have fun planning the trip, figuring out how much it will cost, and how you will gather enough money for it. You will relax on the vacation more if you pay for all of the vacation without putting anything on a credit card or taking out a loan.

81. JEWELRY is one of those things about fashions that can change from year to year. If your style has changed, then it's time to go through your jewelry and give away (or sell online) those pieces you don't want any more.

82. DESIGN a tattoo for yourself. It could be a small one that no one but you will ever see, or a whole arm or foot. If you have a concept but want some help with actually creating it, consider hiring an artist or graphic designer (reputable, with at least 98% positive feedback) from www.fiverr.com. Get it done when you can.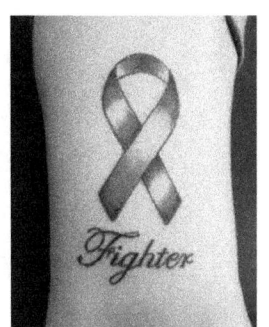

83. LOOK into becoming a mid-wife (helps during the delivery of a baby, focusing on the baby) or a doula (also helps during the delivery of a baby, but focuses on the mom). If it sounds like something you would really like to do, sign up for classes, become an apprentice or take whatever the next step is.

84. CREATE a family budget. There are many samples online to help get you started. Here are eight important steps to create a budget:

    1) Go through all of your receipts and income stubs from the last calendar year. To see where your money is going, organize your receipts into categories and subcategories. Some of those categories can be:
        - Housing (mortgage or rent)
        - Utilities (sewer, trash, electricity, water, etc)
        - Phone, Cable, Internet

- Insurance (homeowners, renters, car, medical, life)
- Vehicle (monthly payment, gas, registration and tags, maintenance)
- Medical and Prescriptions (expenses not covered by insurance)
- Food (restaurants and grocery stores)
- Entertainment / Social (you could add cable in this column if it fits better)
- Miscellaneous (credit card interest, stamps, clothing, toiletries, gifts, haircuts, and so on)
- Home Business (separate these expenses in columns according to your particular business)

2) Organize the stubs from income. Be sure to include money you make from yard sales, selling your chicken's eggs, mowing lawns, babysitting, etc. Remember, this is just for your family to see and use to get a better handle on your finances.

3) Calculate what you spent (expenses) against the money you took in (income).

4) Have a family meeting about money. Lay it all out there. All of the people in the family get a vote, but especially those over 18 and contributing to income (and, of course, those spending money).

5) See where you can cut costs and get out of debt. Make a plan to follow through, including a way to save (more) money.

6) Review your tax forms. See if you can take more deductions in the future, or where you might have made a mistake.

7) Check on your plan on a regular basis. Are you following through? Reducing costs?

85. MEDITATE for ten minutes every day. Trouble calming your mind? Sit quietly with your eyes closed, listening to yourself breathing in and out. Or light a candle at night, and focus on the flicker of the flame.

86. VOW to spend time only with people who make you happy. Work on getting rid of people who are toxic to you, and who make you feel bad about yourself. This includes 'long time friends' and even family members. NO ONE has the right to waste your time and degrade your life.

87. WATCH videos. There are many services you can use to watch those really long movies you've been putting off, or binge-watch the many series available.

88. FIRST aid is becoming a lost skill. Get certified / recertified in first aid and CPR. If you find you have a real passions for helping people feel better, consider becoming a nurse, paramedic, phlebotomist, doctor or someone else in a health-related field.

Boo-Boo Holders

89. TEXT people that you need closure from. Be kind and understanding. Keep it honest but gentle. Write out on a piece of paper ahead of time what you want to say. Don't use short-cut phrases as they could be misinterpreted. Please read and re-read to make sure auto-correct didn't accidentally "correct" something wrong.

90. ALLOCATE a certain amount of money to each of your children, and have them decide where to donate their portion.

91. MAKE a movie, especially if you have other people there with you who are as bored as you. Come up with a simple script, create sets, maybe write a musical score, and start shooting the footage. You can edit the film yourself, or hire it out through possibly www.upwork.com.

92. LEARN to read music.

93. COMPLIMENT yourself every day. Look directly in the mirror (or your reversed camera!) and say one good thing about yourself. Don't just focus on the external… consider saying things like "I love helping people" or "I sing really well".

94. FIND a little something to laugh about each day, too. It could be a meme, a video, a joke your three-year-old tells you, or a comedy show on Netflix.

95. PHOTOS are on our phones these days, but what if something happens to your phone, and you aren't able to access them, or get to your cloud? Now is a great time to download them to a flash / USB / thumb drive. Once you do that, organize them according to topic, such as Scenery, Child 1, Child 2, School, Work, Vacation, Garden, Funny Things, etc. If you find lots of pictures involving other people, like you

have 30-40 with your Aunt, make a copy the photos that involve her onto a thumb drive to give to her on her next birthday or gift-giving holiday. After you have organized your photographs, print out those most special to you, arrange in a special book or picture frame(s), or label and place in your safe.

96. DITTO for your videos.

97. TAKE out a life insurance policy on yourself. Think long and hard about who you want your beneficiary to be.

98. START your own business. So many can be done from home. Write a list of what you do well, and what interests you. Do a little research to find out how much people pay for your service or product in your area (or online). Work out a business plan (samples can be found online). *Note: Take a look at number 152 of this book, which lists a lot of hobbies that you can do for fun and/or to earn money.*

99. HABITS can be good or bad. Did you know it takes a lot of work to change a bad habit? Use this time to get started on that. Click your teeth? MAKE yourself listen for that and snap a rubber band or tug on your earlobe every time you catch yourself doing that. Pick your nose? Put a nasty-smelling / tasting substance (not poisonous, please) on your nose-picking-finger. Always forget to take out the trash? Set an alarm to go off at the same time every time, reminding you to check the trash.

100. DRAWING is something you can't do worth a darn? Time the time now to take lessons, watch how-to videos, and practice. Use pencils or charcoals or even crayons!

101. CHARCUTERIE boards are an art-form ... the arranging of cheeses, ready-to-eat meats, finger foods and a few other things on a platter or board. It can be a small board, or something that reaches across your entire table. Take a variety of meats, cheeses and a few other things to make the most creative charcuterie boards you can come up with, including olives, tiny tomatoes, parsley, radish roses ... try to use only those things that are edible. Then proudly post your pictures.

102. ADOPT or foster a rescue animal, like a cat or dog. If you have the space and facilities, you can even foster reptiles, chickens, alpacas and so on. There are so many animal shelters need your help. Whether or not you are physically able to visit a shelter or take home a critter, you could donate money, purchase feed to be shipped directly there, pay their light bill, or run a campaign to acquire donations.

103. START a spare change jar. Make a plan for the money.... trip, boat, piano, etc.

104. FLOSS every night and if you can, floss after breakfast too.

105. WRITE a book. Whether non-fiction, fiction, a poem or just thoughts ... now is the time to finally get down to writing.

106. TOILET paper was recently in high demand. Some horrible people stockpiled more than they would use in a year, then tried to sell the excess at ridiculous rates. Don't be caught in that cycle. If you come to a time when toilet paper is scarce, make your own.

107. UKULELE players are hard to find. How many people even know what a ukulele is, or how it sounds? Be one of those people who keep that musical instrument alive. Learn how to play. Maybe even give lessons for a bit of extra cash, or hire yourself out as a wedding band.

108. WATCH a sunrise or sunset. You can share the experience even if you can't do it in person (cell phones work great here).

109. MAGAZINES piling up? Have you read all of the back issues to your favorite mag? When will there be a better time than now?!

110. IF you have been holding on to a grudge or bad feeling about someone or situation, consider finally letting go of any negative feelings. You might find yourself feeling better… a little lighter.

111. WRITE a letter to yourself to be opened in five years. Or ten. Or fifty. What do you most want to tell your older self?

112. CARPENTRY is a much needed and in-demand skill. 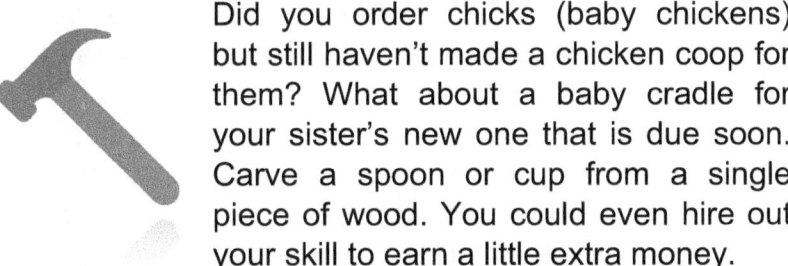 Did you order chicks (baby chickens) but still haven't made a chicken coop for them? What about a baby cradle for your sister's new one that is due soon. Carve a spoon or cup from a single piece of wood. You could even hire out your skill to earn a little extra money.

113. CANDLES are really fun to make. Have you ever wanted to learn how? There are kits that can get you started … from making tea-lights, votives, and tapers. *(Check out YouTube channel '5-Minute Crafts MEN'.)* There are other creative candles, like multi-colored and carving.

114. JOURNAL! Find an empty notebook, or use the computer, and write your thoughts every day. Or use it to track your progress learning languages or recipes or even your weight loss. Log your epilepsy seizures or health symptoms.

115. EXERCISE much? Now is the time to try a new type of exercise. No weights? Use canned goods or paint cans with handles. Try bicycling, ballet, yoga or jogging. Start exercising 5-minutes a day. Then add a second 5-minutes workout to each day. Perhaps increase one of those to 10-minutes, or add yet another 5-minute session.

116. START a scholarship fund in your name, or in the name of a loved one who has passed.

117. CALLIGRAPHY (creating art with the written word) is another skill that is becoming lost. Consider trying it. If you like it, it is a marketable side job, like addressing wedding invitations.

118. LIST twenty things you love about yourself. It could be your clear skin, or your compassion, or your ability to make the best peach-raspberry jam ever tasted.

119. LEARN to cook. Everyone should at least be able to boil water, fry an egg, cook rice or pasta, or cut vegetables. There are videos online, cooking shows, cookbooks (yes, even for super-beginners or children), or you could barter with a friend for cooking lessons in exchange for teaching them something that you do well.

120. SAY "I love you" to someone every day. Yes, saying that to yourself counts but say it to someone else too.

You might bring a smile to someone who was having a really bad day. A genuine smile works wonders too.

121. TEACH your children the value of money, the art of saving, and the compassion of giving. Start out by discussing their allowance: 10 per cent goes here, 20 goes there, 20 is for toys, and so on. Not only will they learn the value of money, but how to budget AND how to do fractions and percentages.

122. PAINT much? Time to finally take that art course you've been putting off. Try water colors, acrylics or oils. Start simple, like mixing colors. Graduate yourself to complicated landscapes or portraits, or explore impressionism.

123. BLOGGING is not quite as popular as it once was, but plenty of people still write and read them. If you feel like you have something to say, start a blog of your own. Two good sites are Blogger or WordPress.

124. UPDATE your resume, especially if you have recently lost your job or been laid off. Even if you can't go looking for a job right now, you will need to at some point. Be prepared. Get help working up the best, most professional resume you can. Then work on your interviewing skills, and organize appropriate interview clothing. Be ready.

125. COMPLETE a puzzle: Don't have any puzzles? Call or 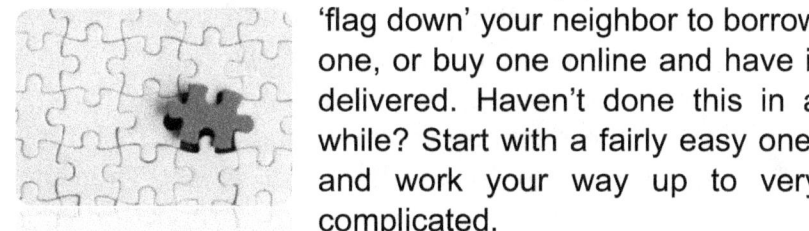 'flag down' your neighbor to borrow one, or buy one online and have it delivered. Haven't done this in a while? Start with a fairly easy one, and work your way up to very complicated.

126. LEARN how to play instrument. There might be musical instrument shops near you that allow you to rent. They might even provide a list of local teachers. YouTube also has videos that could help you learn.

127. COMPLETE a crossword puzzle book... without help!

128. HOW is your sleeping? How many hours of sleep are you getting? Do you feel rested after you have spent time in the bed? Ready for a new day?

129. FRIENDSHIP bracelets can be made either using a kit or scrounging your home for supplies. Make a friendship bracelet for a person in your life who you miss, or use concentrated colors to represent a cause (I do purple for epilepsy awareness). You can find instructions online or a craft book.

130. LETTERS, written on real paper with pen or pencil, and physically mailed, are disappearing from our society in favor of texts or emails. When was the last time you wrote a letter? A real one ... on paper, with ink. Time to get out your fancy paper (or make some!) and write your innermost thoughts to loved ones. Maybe you could use sealing wax, too.

131. TAKE a virtual trip. If you can't physically go around the world to visit the Wonders of the World, then do what you can to take the virtual trip. Decide on a destination, and if you will be "taking" a friend. Learn what you can about the destination, from foods and drinks to clothing to tourist sites to weather, and so on. Then, if you are willing to spend a little, set up a room (or your out-of-

doors patio) to BE the destination. Remember decorations! For instance, for Hawaii, you would have tiki torches, poi, and grass skirts. For Iceland, you might have a room closed off with the air conditioner running hard, and foods would be lamb, dairy and fish.

132. MAKE paper. Paper isn't too difficult to make. My son and I did it as a homeschool project years ago, and I still have the drawing he did on it. You can make paper from old paper you have, plus a blender, a sieve, and a tub. Look up videos on how to make paper out of recycled paper.

133. TRY a food that you never dared to before. It could be a complete dish that you order from a restaurant, or a fruit that someone recommends to you. Supposedly, sometimes we need to try something three times before we can begin to truly appreciate it. Yeah, sorry, but I just can't seem to like Brussels sprouts! *(Pictured: fried chicken feet)*

134. PAY off someone else's debt. You can do this without letting them know YOU did it (anonymously). The amount doesn't have to be large. Perhaps make a payment to the electric company, or use Instacart to buy groceries for someone. Maybe someone is struggling to catch up with rent payments, or the car is about to be repossessed.

135. CLOSET cleaning can suck. When was the last time you wore that outfit in the back of your closet? Has your body shape changed? Styles different? Time to go through everything, try it on, and if you can fit in it AND still like it, keep it. If not, give it away or sell it.

136. SET financial goals, like "become a millionaire" or "buy a farm". Think about it long and hard. Decide the steps you need to take to achieve that goal, and write them all out, in order. Then do them!

137. WORD searches are fun, and can keep your mind active. I did a lot of word search books when I was laid up with my knee replacement surgeries and again recuperating from my first breast cancer surgery. It was a good way to pass the time and keep my mind off of my pain.

138. LEARN how to code. Create your own app, computer program or game.

139. DIET can be such an ugly word, but being confined in your home can cause you to be bored, and then to overeat. Consider giving up the snack foods, processed foods and boredom eating. Plan (and eat) regular meals, being sure to include correct portions of healthy items, like fruits, veggies, nuts and seeds. Limit animal protein to a few times a week (or less).

140. RAZZIE awards are given to movies that were so bad that they needed their own awards. Their actual award is called "the golden raspberry award", pictured. My son would give almost anything to attend one of these award  ceremonies! Through their website at www.razzies.com, you can become a voting member, find out current and past nominees, see who had a good enough sense of humor to accept the award in person, become a sponsor, and through their blog, keep abreast of what is going on. Be sure to watch some of the movies listed as

it could be fun deciding for yourself why the movie was so bad that it was nominated.

141. START a side business to earn money by doing something you are passionate about. *(More listed at number 154.)* These could include:
    - dog washing or walking
    - pet sitting
    - writing
    - entertaining at children's parties as a clown or beloved character or even a character of your own invention
    - making bumper stickers
    - creating one-of-a-kind year-round wreaths for front doors
    - candle-making
    - making hand-sanitizer that has different fragrances

142. PINATAs are fun and aren't just for parties. Make your own. Use a balloon or two and wire hangers to make a  frame, then some old newspapers, baking flour and water to make a paper-mache piñata, making sure to leave a hole to enable you to fill it with goodies. Let dry. Paint and decorate. Fill it with candy (if you have some!), tiny toys, or slips of paper that you've written on ... quotes, prayers ... you decide. Plug up the hole, hang it up, and let the 'whackers' have fun!

143. STAND up and stretch every hour on the hour. This would be a good time to take a drink of water too.

144. BAKE your first loaf of yeast-rising bread. No yeast? Use beer. No beer? Make biscuits with baking powder. No baking powder? Make tortillas!

145. RUBIK'S cube – not just for geeks!

146. VENTRILOQUISM is the skill of "throwing your voice", or making it sound like it is coming from somewhere that is not your mouth. You can learn to do it as a fun thing to bring out at parties, or with a "dummy".

147. THANK you notes and letters are another courtesy that seems to be going the way of the dinosaur. Write a thank you letter to those people who drop off your groceries or other deliveries. Plumbing issues? Slip them a heartfelt THANKS for fixing your toilet. (Tip them too!)

148. MOVIES and TV shows are a go-to choice when you are confined for any length of time. Consider watching an obscure independent film or a foreign subtitled movie. What better time to do this than now?! (Even NETFLIX has movies and series in languages other than English. Try "Ragnarok" or "Always a Witch".)

149. WRITE a song. There are special software programs that can help you on the computer, and special journals and notebooks available with sheet music instead of journal / lined pages.

150. CROCHET something. This is a craft and skill where you use a special hook / needle (that comes in different sizes) and yarn to make fabric, lace, clothing, house decorations, a baby blanket, toaster cozy, washcloth, hats, bags and even toys. My grandmother would use strips cut from bread plastic bags and crochet them into circular rugs. You can take the supplies almost anywhere, like to chemo or even your workplace (during lunch).

151. FIGURE out what the best body weight would be for you. Is it attainable? Would it be healthy? Develop a plan to healthfully get to that weight. Take into account what you eat, your activity level, medications that might be messing with your appetite or adding water weight. Discuss with a nutritionist or diet specialist to formulate a workable and realistic plan. Maybe even get a diet-buddy (help each other).

152. GET to know your neighbors, by keeping a safe distance, or if you are snow-bound, use walkie-talkies or large signs (or Post-It™ notes) in windows.

153. ETSY is a great place to shop, but even more, it is a great website to sell the products of your own creation. Favorites sold include: special soap, jewelry, carved candles, hand-drawn greeting cards, and home décor.

154. HOBBIES are mentioned in other places in this book, but I thought I would make a more comprehensive list here. Some of these can be done at home, when you are bored, and some you need to leave the house to do. You can turn many of these into a good way to earn income, if you desire... ... *(Those marked with an * are hobbies you can turn into a good way to earn income, if you desire. Be sure to research the skill/hobby, and do all the appropriate steps to be a legal business in your area.)*

   1) 3D printing *
   2) Acrobatics
   3) Acting *
   4) Acupressure *
   5) Acupuncture *
   6) Alternative Power System Developing *

7) Amateur Radio

8) Animation *

9) Aquascaping

10) Archery

11) Astrology *

12) Astronomy

13) Backpacking Prep or Consulting *

14) Backyard chicken or quail farmer (sell eggs) *

15) Backyard gardener of food/produce, herbs, or flowers (sell your extras) *

16) Backyard rabbit farmer (raise the rabbits for meat for your household but you can sell the rabbit poop as fertilizer that doesn't first need composting. *

17) Baking (find out what is allowed in your area by looking up the "cottage law".) *

18) Basket Weaving *

19) Baton Twirling

20) Beekeeping Research

21) Birdwatching

22) Blogging *

23) Board-Game Playing and Competitions

24) Bonsai Gardening

25) Book Narrator *

26) Book Restoration *

27) Bowling

28) Breadmaking *

29) Building *

30) Bullet-Journaling

31) Bushcraft Consulting *
32) Butterfly Watching
33) Candy Making *
34) Car Fixing and Building *
35) Card Games
36) Ceramics *
37) Cheesemaking
38) Clothesmaking *
39) Coffee Roasting
40) Collages

41) Collecting (stamps, buttons, coins, seeds, comic books, die-cast toys, action figures, dolls, perfume, movie memorabilia, rocks, shoes, sports things, tickets, toys, vintage cars, vintage clothing, vinyl records, etc)
42) Coloring
43) Computer Programming *
44) Cosplaying
45) Coupon Clipping
46) Creating Coloring Pages and Books *
47) Creative Writing
48) Cross-Stitch and Counted Cross-Stitch *
49) Crossword Puzzles
50) Cryptography
51) Dance
52) Dance Instruction *
53) Digital Arts
54) DJing *
55) Dominoes
56) Dowsing (*pic* ➡) *
57) Drink-Mixing / Bartending *

58) Editing for Voice-Overs and Book Narrations *
59) Electronic Games
60) Electronics
61) Fantasy Sports
62) Fashion Consultant *
63) Fashion Design *
64) Fishkeeping
65) Flower Arranging *
66) Fly Tying *
67) Food Forest and Permaculture Design *
68) Furniture Building / Carpentry *
69) Genealogy *
70) Gingerbread House Making (and Competing)
71) Glassblowing *
72) Graphic Design *
73) Gunsmithing
74) Gymnastics
75) Hacking (NOT recommending you break the law!) *
76) HAM radio
77) Home Improvement *
78) Homebrewing
79) Houseplant care
80) Hula Hooping
81) Hydroponics
82) Ice Skating
83) Jam and Jelly Maker (again, refer to your local "cottage law".) *
84) Jewelry Design and Jewelry-Making *
85) Juggling *

86) Karaoke
87) Karate
88) Knife Making *
89) Knot Tying
90) Lace Making *
91) Leather Crafting *
92) LEGOs™ building
93) Lock Picking (I am NOT recommending you break the law!) *
94) Macramé
95) Magic Tricks *
96) Makeup
97) Makeup for other people for special occasions, like prom or weddings*
98) Makeup Tutorials
99) Maze creator *
100) Metalworking *
101) Millinery *
102) Model Car Building
103) Mystery / Secret Shopper *
104) Nail Art *
105) Needlepoint *
106) Numerology *
107) Origami
108) Painting *
109) Palmistry *
110) Pet Adoption and Fostering
111) Photography *
112) Ping-Pong / Table Tennis
113) Pottery *

114) Powerlifting
115) Practical Jokes
116) Pressed Flowers
117) Psychic Skills *
118) Puzzles of all kinds, including jigsaw
119) Quilling *
120) Quilting *
121) Quizzes
122) Rail Transport Modeling
123) Rapping
124) Reading
125) Refinishing *
126) Reflexology *
127) Reiki *
128) Scrapbooking
129) Sculpting *
130) Sewing *
131) Shoemaking *
132) Singing
133) Sketching
134) Soapmaking *
135) Social Media Influencer *
136) Stand-Up Comic *
137) Stop-Motion Film-Making *
138) Tarot Cards *
139) Taxidermy *
140) Therapeutic Touch *
141) Thrifting
142) Video Editing *

143) Video Game Developing *
144) Video Gaming
145) Voice-Over Actor *
146) Waxing
147) Weaving on a Loom
148) Weight Training
149) Welding *
150) Whittling *
151) Wikipedia Editing
152) Wine-Making
153) Wood Carving / Woodworking *
154) Word Searches
155) Worldbuilding
156) Writer *
157) Yoga *
158) Yo-Yo Tricks
159) Zumba Instructor *

155. CREATE a medical information sheet. Because my son and I have complicated health issues, we carry an updated "medical information sheet" with us everywhere. This is a good time to create one for you and others in your household. For the form, see the next page.

The Bored Book ... 155 Things To Do

"Medical Information Sheet"

Page 1 of 2

Full Name:	
Prefers to be called:	
Current Address and Cell Phone / Contact Information:	
Birthdate ___/___/___	
Allergic to (☐Medicine / ☐Other):	Reaction:
Allergic to (☐Medicine / ☐Other):	Reaction:
Allergic to (☐Medicine / ☐Other):	Reaction:
Allergic to (☐Medicine / ☐Other):	Reaction:
Allergic to (☐Medicine / ☐Other):	Reaction:
Allergic to (☐Medicine / ☐Other):	Reaction:
Emergency Contact: Name, Relationship and Phone	
Primary care physician name/practice/address/phone/fax:	
Pharmacy name/address/phone:	

Notes:

Name: _____   Page 2 of 2

My current medications (for any purpose) (name, dosage, frequency):
My OTC (Over-The-Counter) Supplements:
My health history/What I have been diagnosed with and when, and what medications tried:
Family health history (who has [or had] what):
Surgeries including when, where, why:
Hospitalizations and dates:

Notes:

CHAPTER THREE: ACTIVITY PAGES

The following are pages for you to color, compose a poem, solve a word search or do some creative writing.

The backs of most of the coloring pages are left blank in case you want to use paint, markers, or even rip out to decorate and frame.

Enjoy!

Vikki Lawrence

Color This Page

Vikki Lawrence

Writing Prompt
Compose a poem that includes these three words:
Jungle
Sift
Kitten

The Bored Book ... 155 Things To Do

Color This Page

Color This Page

What does LOVE look like to you:

_____

_____

_____

_____

_____

_____

_____

The Bored Book ... 155 Things To Do

Vikki Lawrence

Writing Prompt
Compose a poem that includes these three words:
Purple
Introduce
Snow

Color This Page

Writing Prompt

Use the next four pages to compose a short story that includes these five words:

Casino
Zinc
Intervene
Footwork
Mold

Your Story Title Is:_____

Color This Page

Vikki Lawrence

Word Search : "VISION BOARD"

```
                  C R R S P B F G
                N R A E L P I E O T R Q
              N O T E S O I H C E J P O J
            S E I R     M R S A     E Q W J
          J U C T E     O I N P     R V S T R
          O C N A T     T T O S     F I M S H
      R P O A R R       O U I D     O S Y L N W
      X I F N I E       R A T E     R U Y M O I
      Y C R I P A       C L A R     M A P O I M
      G T I F S T O J Y I L C M C A L P T T P
      R U E Z N A M V C T E A A A N I A I A R
      E R N G I O E O L Y R S W R C Z H V C O
      N E D   O B M I E Y O J N E E E   A A V
      E S S     A S T I C K E R E N     T V E
        F H X     L S A Y I N G R     H I   E
        L I R V                       O Q O S
          P L S X                   M U O N
            S O C I A L L I F E E O X L
              P V Y H T L A E H T T O
                E E M P O W E R
```

Search for the following words:

Boat	Growth	Memo	Sacred
Car	Happy	Motivation	Space
Career	Healthy	Motorcycle	Saying
Empower	Home	Notes	Social Life
Energy	Improve	Performance	Spirituality
Enjoy	Inspiration	Pictures	Sticker
Finance	Job	Quote	Vacation
Focus	Learn	Relationship	Visualize
Friendship	Life	Retreat	
Goal	Love	RV	

Answers are at the back of this book.

What will YOUR vision board have on it?

Vikki Lawrence

Color This Page

Vikki Lawrence

Color This Page

Don't worry. Just smile!

Word Search : "GARDEN BEAUTY"

```
            B Y Q
          D L N J S
          S P O A G
    S G   H I E S U     P O
A   I U L   L P T     U Y R P
S   D O N A W Q E   C A L I L
A   X A Z F B O R Y S N A P
    S A H   L E R   Z M A
          L T O N R
  I E B T I N W I A Q   U
  N F U P   A   E S Y   Z
  A B F X   V   T R X   E
    A J     S     D O
            A
            L
            V
            I
            A
            Y
            L
            I
M T U L I P L Y A T S O H
  D L O G I R A M K A K
  Q H I B I S C U S P B
  S I R I A I N O G E B
  N O I T A N R A C W G
  C R O C U S S E S O R
    B L U E B E L L E
    A E G N A R D Y H
```

Search for the following words:

Aster
Azalea
Begonia
Bluebell
Buttercup
Carnation
Crocus
Dahlia
Hibiscus
Hosta
Hydrangea
Iris
Lilac
Lily
Marigold
Pansy
Peony
Phlox
Rose
Salvia
Sunflower
Tulip
Yarrow

Answers are at the back of this book

Writing Prompt

Use the next four pages to compose a short story that includes these five words:

Twenty-two
Surgery
Audio
Cow
Parsnip

Your Story Title Is:_____

The Bored Book … 155 Things To Do

Vikki Lawrence

Color This Page

TAKE PRECAUTIONS

Word Search : "BE BUSY"

```
                  L  E  A  T  H  E  R  G
                  T  G  E  S  R  D  N
               J  N  T  D  E  A  I
               I  I  R  P  N  K
            S  R  A  A  C  A
            W  C  P  E  M  S
               G  S  R  R  R  I
               R  E  E  O  Y
               D  E  W  L  R  O
               B  O  O  E  O
         J     L  C  T  T
         F     G  T  T
               O  A  B  N
         P     T  S  E
         S     P  D
         O     R
      M  A
      G  P
         C
   G
```

Search for the following words:		
Beermaking	Leather	Sing
Cards	Mop	Soap
Color	Paint	Tattoo
Dance	Paper	Write
Flowers	Pottery	
Garden	Sew	

Answers are at the back of this book.

Vikki Lawrence

Color This Page
Do A Random Act of Kindness

Vikki Lawrence

Writing Prompt
Compose a poem that includes these three words:
Jungle
Sift
Kitten

Vikki Lawrence

Color This Page
DON'T GIVE UP HOPE

Dear Reader:

Thank you for buying this book. Please leave a review on the Amazon page or at Goodreads.

Meanwhile, I hope you will take the time to check out some of my other published works.

V.P. Lawrence

MORE BOOKS

I plan to release additional books about getting ready for certain situations in life. These will hopefully include:

- Get Ready For ManMade Events
- Get Ready For Natural Disasters
- Get Ready For Personal Challenges
- Get Ready For Political B.S.
- Get Ready For The Zombies and Mutants!
- Get Ready To Manage Health Circumstances
- How To Eat From Your Pantry
- How To Grow Your Food
- How To Make Healthy Homemade MREs
- How to Raise Animals for Food
- The Bored Book: 155 Things To Do

About the Author

V.P. Lawrence grew up in Louisville, KY but has lived many places in the United States. She's an avid reader (from non-fiction to fantasy, thrillers, and most genres in between) who became a writer/author.

As much as she hated to leave her little goat and chicken farm in Colorado, she and her son, Weslee, moved back to Louisville to be near family and dear old friends.

Weslee (pictured) is an autistic adult with uncontrolled epilepsy.

CONTACT INFORMATION

Publisher Blog
www.vikki-lawrence.blogspot.com

Fiction
www.v-lawrence-author.blogspot.com

Journals/Calendars
www.ria-pearce.blogspot.com

Non-Fiction – Seizures / Epilepsy
www.seizures-suck.blogspot.com

Non-Fiction – Preparing For Disasters
www.survival-cooking.blogspot.com

Facebook
www.facebook.com/AuthorVikkiLawrence

Instagram-Epilepsy and Personal
@vikkilawrence1

Instagram-Prepping
@survivalcookingliving

Amazon Author Page
www.amazon.com/-/e/B00LFVUGC0

FIVE YEAR PREP JOURNALS / DIARIES

The following are four journals / diaries for people who prepare for emergency or crisis situations, that can range from power outages, drought, infrastructure or financial collapse, pandemic, and more. Use to track skills learned, items or skills to barter, things stored, and more.

www.amazon.com/dp/1691500607/

www.amazon.com/dp/1691494836/
/

www.amazon.com/dp/1691442763/

www.amazon.com/dp/1691310972

BLANK FIVE-YEAR JOURNALS / DIARIES

The following are links to some blank journals.

https://www.amazon.com/dp/1709692073

https://www.amazon.com/dp/1708756213

https://www.amazon.com/dp/1689821558

https://www.amazon.com/dp/1689581654

https://www.amazon.com/dp/1689659289

https://www.amazon.com/dp/1689812567

https://www.amazon.com/dp/1688595880

https://www.amazon.com/dp/1691296201

https://www.amazon.com/dp/1690197161

Writing Prompt Books

The following are five writing prompt workbooks, good for budding writers, people who have writer's block, and even students.

https://www.amazon.com/dp/1885615132

https://www.amazon.com/dp/1885615159

https://www.amazon.com/dp/1885615167

https://www.amazon.com/dp/1885615175

https://www.amazon.com/dp/1885615108

FIVE-YEAR SEIZURE DIARIES / TRACKERS

The following are some journals people like my son use to track seizures and other things related to their seizure disorder / epilepsy.

https://www.amazon.com/dp/1710350008

https://www.amazon.com/dp/1694810488

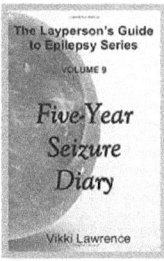

https://www.amazon.com/dp/171036243X

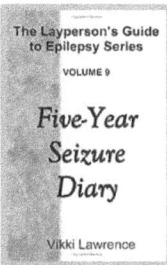

https://www.amazon.com/dp/1694813991

https://www.amazon.com/dp/1710359633

/

NOTES

NOTES

NOTES

Notes

NOTES

NOTES

NOTES

Answers

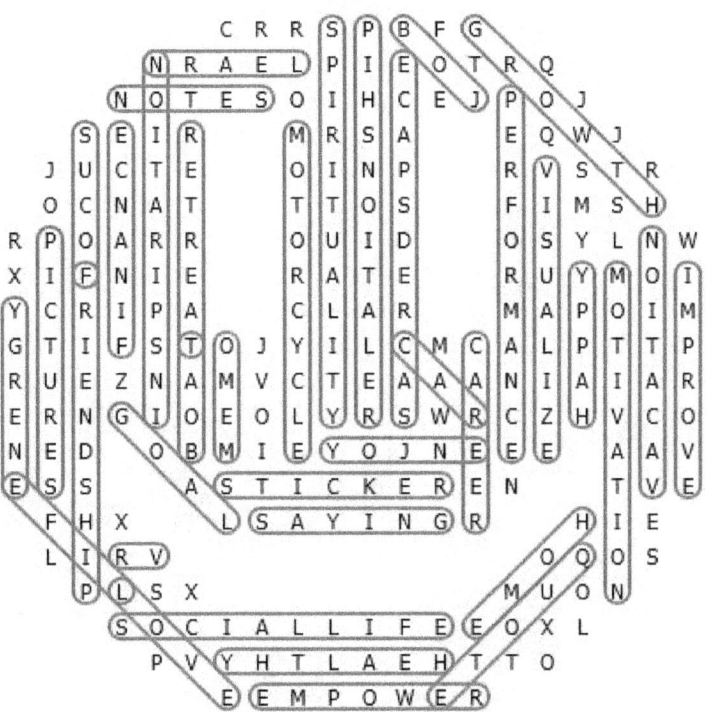

Answers for "Vision Board"

The Bored Book ... 155 Things To Do

Answers

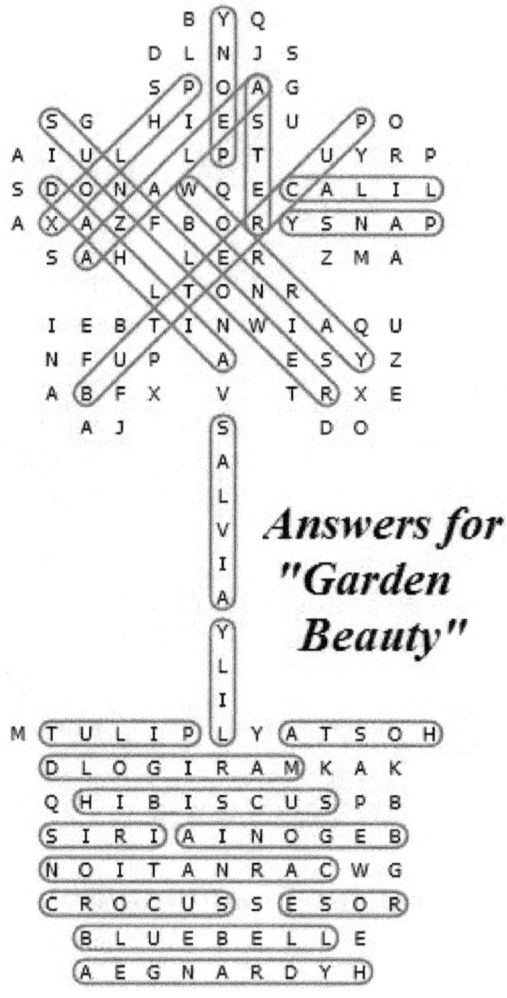

Answers for "Garden Beauty"

Vikki Lawrence

Answers

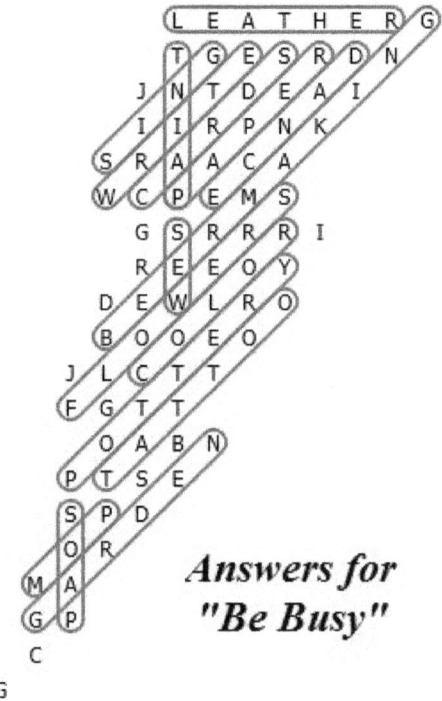

Answers for "Be Busy"

www.ingramcontent.com/pod-product-compliance
Lightning Source LLC
Chambersburg PA
CBHW071720040426
42446CB00011B/2148